Lunch Box Revolution

Revolution

Recipes for a proper lunch

Gil Kahana / Michiko Nitta

What is this book?

This book is about your life. More specifically, it is about your lunch.

Often skipped or rushed, your lunch is more important than you think.

With this book, we would like to inspire you to bring your own lunchbox to work.

Our recipes are designed for people with a busy life style who can't spend too much time in the kitchen,

but want to improve the way they eat.

We hope you will give it a try,

and that it will enable you to create lunchboxes to be proud of!

Who are we?

Gil is a foodie who is also responsible for creating innovative and engaging user experience.

Michiko is a visual artist & interaction designer who grew up in Japan, the country famous for it's creative lunch box culture.

While working in a design studio, they discovered their shared passion for home made food
and decided to create this book, hoping it will inspire other people to make their own lunchboxes.

Our recipes follow 3 simple principles:

1. Easy to make by following simple instructions.

2. Tasty, sometimes even tastier on the day after...

3. Made from affordable ingredients that are easy to find.

What you will need:

Our recipes require basic kitchen utensils only (no blenders are needed...)

Be brave:

If you are not sure about something, just give it a try your way !

Proper lunch manifesto

We are busy but know how important it is to take a proper
lunch break.

No previous cooking experience is required.
Everyone can do it!

We take pride in our lunchbox– we make our own food which
tastes better and costs less!

The wrong idea of lunch ...

- A sandwich in front of your computer
- Potato chips
- Eating during a meeting ...

Why should you take a proper lunch?

Because you will be
more productive!

Because it will make
you healthier!

Because it will
be more socially
engaging!

before → after

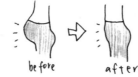

Show me
your
lunch box!

Five elements theory in Chinese cooking: Yin & Yang
Easy way to cook healthy, tasty and beautiful meals

In Chinese culture, food is believed to have medicinal properties. Attributes such as color, aroma and flavor are equally important when making a dish.
Simply giving attention to combine three to five colors per dish, selected from ingredients that are green, red, yellow, white, black/caramel colored, helps to create a healthy diet.
It may sound difficult to do, however five colors can be found in everyday ingredients shown below.

Lunch box recipes

Meat balls

with couscous

2 portions
preparation: 20 minutes
cooking: 25 minutes

Ingredients

1x Egg
beaten

1x Medium onion
finely chopped

4x Garlic cloves
peeled & crushed

Ketchup
1 tbsp

A handful of parsley
finely chopped

Paprika
1 tsp

Cumin powder
1 tsp

Bread
½ slice

Minced beef
200g/ 7oz

Olive oil
3 tbsp

Chopped tomatoes
230g/ 8oz tin

1x Medium tomato
finely chopped

Water
90ml/ 3 fl. oz

Couscous
to serve

Process

1. In a large bowl, put the egg, onion, half of the garlic, ketchup, parsley paprika and cumin powder.

2. Soak the bread in water, then squeeze to drain. Break it into small pieces and add to bowl.

3. Mix in minced beef until well com-bined. Season with salt and pepper to taste.

4. Wet your hands and form small balls from the mixture.

5. In a large pan, heat the olive oil over high heat, then carefully add the meatballs.

6. Fry the meatballs for 3 minutes on each side, then remove from pan.

7. Place the tinned and fresh tomatoes, water and the remaining garlic in a saucepan.

8. Season with salt and pepper to taste.

9. Gently place the meatballs inside the saucepan and bring to boil.

10. Simmer over medium heat for 15 minutes. Meanwhile prepare couscous according to packet instructions.

In your lunchbox arrange a layer of couscous and top with a portion of the meatballs.

HAM ROLL BENTO

■ 2 portions   ■ preparation: 15 minutes   ■ Cooking: 13 minutes

Ingredients:

Green beans
200g/ 7oz, trimmed

1x Small sweet potato
peeled & cubed

1x Medium potato
peeled & cubed

Olive oil
4 tbsp

Greek yogurt
2 tbsp

Mayonnaise
2 tbsp

20g/ 1oz Walnuts
finely chopped

¼ Small onion
finely chopped

A handful of parsley
finely chopped

Cooked ham
6 slices

6x Cherry tomatoes

Process:

1. Cook the green beans in boiling water for 3 minutes. Drain and leave to cool.

2. Cook the potato and sweet potato in boiling water for 10 minutes or until tender. Drain and leave to cool.

3. Make the potato salad. In a large bowl prepare the dressing by whisking the olive oil, yogurt, mayonnaise, walnuts, onion and parsley.

4. Mix in the potato and sweet potato. Season with salt and pepper to taste.

5. Wrap 6 green beans tightly in a slice of ham.

6. Gently cut the roll into 2 pieces with a sharp knife.

7. Repeat the process until you have used all the ham slices.

In your lunchbox arrange the potato salad, rolled ham and cherry tomatoes.

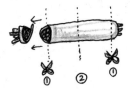

VEGETABLE Curry

♥ 2 portions ♣ preparation : 20 minutes ♦ cooking : 30 minutes

Ingredients:

Olive oil
2 tbsp

2x Cardamom pods
crushed

Turmeric
1 tsp

Cumin powder
1 tsp

1x Medium onion
finely chopped

3x Garlic cloves
peeled & crushed

Root ginger
1 tbsp, grated

*
1x Red chilli
finely chopped

1x Small sweet potatos
peeled & cubed

1x Courgette
roughly chopped

1x Red pepper
roughly chopped

Water
220ml/ 7.5 fl. oz

Basmati rice
to serve

½ Bunch coriander
finely chopped

Coconut milk
90 ml/ 3 fl. oz

Process:

1. Heat oil in a saucepan.

2. Fry the cardamom pods, turmeric and cumin for 1 minute.

3. Add the onion, garlic, ginger, chilli and sweet potato. Stir for two minutes.

4. Add the courgette and red pepper. Stir-fry for further two minutes.

5. Add the water and bring to boil. Simmer for 15 minutes or until vegetables are tender. Meanwhile prepare the rice according to packet instructions.

6. Mix in the coriander and coconut milk. Season with salt and pepper.

7. Remove from heat and allow to cool.

In your lunchbox arrange a layer of rice and top with a curry portion.

* Deseed the chilli if you want it to be less spicy.

Beef Stroganoff

☆ portions: **2**
☆ preparation: **15** minutes
☆ cooking: **25** minutes

Ingredients:

80g/3oz New potatoes
halved

Olive oil
2 tbsp

350g/ 12oz Rump steak
cut into strips

Butter
25g/1oz

1x Medium onion
finely chopped

2x Garlic cloves
peeled & crushed

Ground paprika
1 tsp

80g/3oz Mushrooms
quartered

1x Red pepper
roughly chopped

Flour
1 tbsp

Water
200ml/7 fl. oz

Lemon juice
1 tbsp

Worcester sauce
1 tbsp

A handful of parsley
finely chopped

Sour cream
100ml/3 fl. oz

Process:

1. Cook the new potatoes in boiling water for 15 minutes. Drain and put aside.

2. Heat the olive oil in a frying pan over high heat.

3. Stir-fry the steak strips until golden-brown. Remove from frying pan and put aside.

4. Heat the butter in the same frying pan.

5. Stir in the onion, garlic, paprika and new potatoes. Cook for 4 minutes over medium heat.

6. Add the mushrooms, red pepper, flour and cook for 2 minutes until the mushrooms are soft.

7. Add the water, lemon juice, Worcester sauce and bring to boil, stirring.

8. Add the parsley and season with salt and pepper to taste.

9. Return the meat to the frying pan, add the sour cream and simmer for 6 minutes until the meat is fully cooked.

In your lunchbox arrange a portion of the beef stroganoff.

Bulgur & Halloumi Salad

※ 2 portions　　※ preparation: 15 minutes　　※ cooking: 15 minutes

Ingredients

Olive oil
2 tbsp

Halloumi cheese
150g/5oz, sliced

Bulgur wheat
100g/3.5 oz

Water
220ml/ 7.5 fl. oz

Canned chickpeas
200g/ 7oz, rinsed

1x Spring onion
sliced

6x Radishes
sliced

1x Stalk celery
sliced

Sesami oil
2 tbsp

Lemon juice
4 tbsp

Ground cumin
1 tsp

Paprika
1 tsp

Process

1. Heat oil in a frying pan.

2. Fry the halloumi cheese on both sides until golden, then put aside.

3. Rinse the bulgur wheat. Drain and place in a saucepan with the water.

4. Bring the bulgur to boil. Simmer for 10 minutes until soft. Allow to cool.

5. In a large bowl add the bulgur wheat, halloumi cheese, chickpeas, spring onion, radishes and celery.

6. Add the sesame oil, lemon juice, cumin and paprika. Season with salt and pepper to taste.

In your lunchbox arrange a portion of the bulgar and halloumi salad.

Ginger chicken & salad

* 2 portions *** preparation: 20 minutes** *** cooking: 10 minutes**

Ingredients

White wine
60ml/ 2 fl. oz

Sugar
2 tbsp

Soy sauce
5 tbsp

Root ginger
2 tbsp, grated

2x chicken breasts
cut into strips

Olive oil
6 tbsp

1x Large onion
finely chopped

5x mushrooms
quartered

White wine vinegar
1 tbsp

½ Cucumber
diced

2x Carrots
peeled & diced

Cooked rice
to serve

Process

1. In a bowl, mix the white wine, sugar, soy sauce and ginger.

2. Add the chicken strips and marinate for at least 10 minutes.

3. Heat 3 tbsp olive oil in a frying pan.

4. Stir-fry the onion for 2 minutes or until it begins to soften.

5. Add the chicken with it's marinade and stir fry for 5 minutes until the chicken strips are opaque.

6. Lower the heat, then stir in the mushrooms.

7. Cover and simmer for 3 minutes. Remove from heat.

8. Make the salad dressing by mixing 3 tbsp olive oil with the vinegar. Season with salt and pepper to taste. Pack in a small container.

In your lunchbox arrange the diced cucumber and carrots in one compartment and a layer of rice topped with the ginger chicken in the other.

Don't forget to take your salad dressing...

AFRICAN RICE

portions: **2**
preparation: **10**minutes
cooking: **20**minutes

Ingredients

Rice
200g/7oz

Olive oil
4 tbsp

1x Onion
finely chopped

4x Garlic cloves
peeled & crushed

1x Red chilli
finely chopped

150g/5oz Cauliflower
Cut into small florets

Peanut butter
2 tbsp

1x Large tomato
finely chopped

Tomato puree
1 tbsp

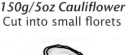

Water
200ml/7 fl. oz

Spinach
150g/ 5oz

Process

1. Cook the rice following the packet instructions. Meanwhile, heat the olive oil in a large pan.

2. Stir in the onion, garlic, chilli and cauliflower. Fry for 4 minutes over high heat.

3. Add the peanut butter, tomato, tomato puree and water. Simmer for 7 minutes.

4. Stir in the cooked rice and spinach. Remove from heat and leave to cool.

In your lunchbox arrange a portion of the African rice.

*Deseed the chilli if you want it to be less spicy.

Happosai

portions: 2
preparation: 30 minutes
Cooking: 7 minutes

Ingredients

Fine egg noodle
150g/ 5oz

Sesame oil
3 tbsp

½ Chicken stock cube

Water
50ml/ 2 fl. oz, boiling

White wine
50ml/ 2oz

Hot chilli paste
2 tsp

Sunflower oil
1 tbsp

1x Garlic clove
finely chopped

2x Spring onions
finely sliced

Pork mince
150g/ 5oz

Root ginger
2 tbsp, grated

½ Carrot
cut into sticks

5x Mushrooms
Sliced

3x Cabbage leaves
roughly chopped

Raw prawns
100g/ 3oz

Process

1. Cook the egg noodles in boiling water for 1 minute. Drain and then drizzle with sesame oil to prevent sticking.

2. Make the sauce. In a small bowl, dissolve 1/2 chicken cube stock with the boiling water.

3. Mix in the white wine and hot chilli paste.

4. Heat the sunflower oil in a large frying pan or wok over high heat.

5. Add the garlic, spring onions and pork mince. Stir fry, breaking up any lumps, until the mince is lightly brown.

6. Add the ginger, carrot and mushrooms. Stir well for 30 seconds.

7. Stir in the cabbage leaves and prawns. Pour the sauce and stir lightly.

8. Lower to medium heat, cover with a lid and simmer for 2 minutes.

9. Take the lid off, stir lightly.

In your lunchbox arrange a portion of the Happosai.

Penne, Rose

* portions: **2**
* preparation: 15 minutes
* cooking: 30 minutes

Ingredients

Penne pasta
200g/ 7oz

Olive oil
3 tbsp

1x Medium onion
finely chopped

Pancetta cubes
50g/ 2oz

2x Medium tomatoes
finely chopped

Ketchup
2 tbsp

Water
90ml/ 3 fl. oz

Double cream
90ml/ 3 fl. oz

Process

1. Cook the penne according to packet instructions. Meanwhile heat the olive oil in a large frying pan.

2. Add the onion and pancetta cubes. Fry for 5 minutes until the onion is soft.

3. Stir in the tomatoes, ketchup and water. Cook for 10 minutes until the sauce is thick.

4. Mix in the double cream. Season with salt and pepper to taste.

5. Add drained penne to the frying pan and stir over low heat for 2 minutes. Remove from heat and allow to cool.

In your lunchbox arrange a portion of the penne rose.

Potato Gratin
with warm veggies

2 portions   preparation: 10 minutes   cooking: 30 minutes

Ingredients

2x Large potatoes
peeled

Olive oil
1 tbsp

1x Garlic clove
peeled & crushed

Double cream
75ml/ 2.5 fl. oz

Milk
75ml/ 2.5 fl. oz

A pinch of nutmeg

Cheddar cheese
40g/ 1.5 oz, grated

60g/ 2oz Broccoli
cut into small florets

5x Radishes

Process

1. Preheat the oven to 170C / 325F/ Gas mark 3.

2. Slice the potatoes very thinly and rinse under cold water. Drain well.

3. Grease a small oven proof dish with the olive oil and garlic.

4. Layer the potatoes inside the oven proof dish.

5. In a small bowl, mix the double cream, milk and nutmeg. Season with salt and pepper to taste.

6. Pour the bowl mixture over the top of the layered potatoes.

7. Sprinkle the grated cheese on top.

8. Bake in the oven for 1 hour. Meanwhile, cook the broccoli and radishes in boiling water for 3 minutes, remove from heat and drain well.

In your lunchbox, arrange a portion of the gratin with some broccoli and radish on the side.

Smoked Fish

with Salad

2 portions   preparation : 5 minutes   cooking : 10 minutes

Ingredients

2x Carrots
ribboned

Sea salt
2 tbsp

Olive oil
3 tbsp

A handful of parsley
finely chopped

Green beans
200g/ 7oz

100g/3oz Baby corn
halved lengthwise

English mustard
1 tsp

Smoked mackerel fillet
100g/ 3oz, skinned

Bread
to serve

Process

Carrot salad

1. Put the ribboned carrots in a bowl. Sprinkle with sea salt and mix well. Let stand for 2 minutes to soften.

2. Rinse the carrots then squeeze out any excess water.

3. Season with 2 tbsp olive oil, black pepper and parsley. Mix well.

Beans and baby corn salad

1. Cook the green beans and baby corn for 3 minutes in boiling, salted water. Drain well.

2. In a bowl, mix 1 tbsp olive oil with the mustard.

3. Mix in the green beans and baby corn.

4. Season with salt and pepper to taste.

In your lunchbox, arrange the smoked mackerel and both salads.

Chicken Drumsticks

+

Beans & Peas Salad

2portions   preparation:1hour marination +10minutes   cooking:30minutes

Ingredients

4x Chicken drumsticks

Olive oil
4 tbsp

Soy sauce
2 tbsp

Honey
1 tbsp

2x Garlic cloves
peeled & crushed

Sesame seeds
1 tbsp

Frozen broad beans
200g/ 7oz, defrosted

Frozen peas
200g/ 7oz, defrosted

Lemon juice
2 tbsp

Fresh mint
2 tbsp, chopped

Fresh basil
2 tbsp, chopped

Process

Chicken drumsticks

1. Preheat the oven to 180C / 350F/ Gas mark 4

2. Score the drumsticks deeply with a sharp knife.

3. In a plastic bag, make the marinade by mixing 2 tbsp olive oil, soy sauce, honey and 1 clove garlic. Season with black pepper to taste.

4. Add the drumsticks to the marinade and leave to marinate for 1 hour.

5. Place the chicken drumsticks in a greased ovenproof dish, sprinkle with the sesame seeds. Keep some of the marinade in the plastic bag.

6. Bake for 15 minutes, baste with remaining marinade and then continue baking for a further 15 minutes.

7. Remove from oven and let cool.

Broad beans salad

1. Place broad beans and peas in a bowl.

2. Add the remaining olive oil, garlic clove, lemon juice, mint and basil.

3. Season with salt & pepper and mix together.

In your lunchbox arrange the chicken drumsticks with the broad bean salad.

Chicken & Broccoli
Rigatoni

2 portions   preparation : 15 minutes   cooking : 30 minutes

Ingredients

Rigatoni pasta
200g/ 7oz

Olive oil
3 tbsp

1x Red onion
finely chopped

3x Garlic cloves
peeled & crushed

1x Red chilli
finely chopped

1x Chicken breast
diced

120g/ 4oz Broccoli
cut into small florets

1x Red pepper
roughly chopped

Crème fraîche
100ml/ 3 fl. oz

Cheddar cheese
50g/ 2oz, grated

1x Bunch fresh basil
shredded

Process

1. Cook the rigatoni pasta according to packet instructions. Meanwhile, heat the oil in a large saucepan.

2. Add the onion, garlic and chilli. Stir for 3 minutes over high heat.

3. Add the chicken, broccoli and red pepper. Stir for about 5 minutes until the chicken is lightly golden.

4. Season with salt and pepper to taste.

5. Mix in the crème fraîche, cheddar and rigatoni pasta. Remove from heat.

6. Sprinkle with the shredded basil.

In your lunchbox, arrange a portion of the rigatoni.

*Deseed the chilli if you want it to be less spicy.

❧ Stir fried ❧
Thai noodle

❧ 2portions ❧ preparation: 20minutes ❧ cooking: 15minutes

Ingredients

fine egg noodles
150g/ 5oz

Sesame oil
2 tbsp

½ Chicken stock cube

Water
50ml/ 2 fl. oz, boiling

Oyster sauce
1 tbsp

Thai fish sauce
1 tbsp

Sugar
1 tbsp

Sunflower oil
3 tbsp

2x Eggs
beaten

1x Chicken breast
cut into strips

1x Onion
thinly sliced

1x Garlic clove
peeled & crushed

1x Red chilli
deseeded & sliced

1x Red pepper
cut into sticks

10x Basil leaves
roughly chopped

1x Bunch coriander
finely chopped

Process

1. Cook the noodles in boiling water for 1 minute. Drain and then drizzle with sesame oil to prevent sticking.

2. Make the sauce in a bowl.
Dissolve the chicken stock cube with the water. Mix in the oyster sauce, fish sauce and sugar. Set aside.

3. Heat 1 tbsp of the sunflower oil in a large frying pan or wok. Add the eggs and cook, stirring, until scrambled. Remove from pan and put aside.

4. Heat the remaining sunflower oil in the same frying pan or wok.

5. Stir-fry the chicken breast and onion over a high heat for 4 minutes.

6. Add the garlic, red chilli and red pepper. Stir for 2 minutes.

7. Stir in the basil, coriander, noodles and sauce. Cook for 2 minutes until the chicken is cooked through. Season with black pepper to taste.

In your lunchbox, arrange a portion of the Thai noodles and top with the scrambled eggs.

ROASTED veggies

2 portions   preparation: 15 minutes   cooking: 30 minutes

Ingredients

2x Small onions
peeled & quartered

2x Small beetroots
peeled & quartered

2x Small parsnips
peeled & quartered

2x Small carrots
peeled & quartered

New potatoes
200g/ 7oz, halved

Olive oil
5 tbsp

Balsamic vinegar
4 tsp

Honey
4 tsp

6x Garlic clove
peeled & crushed

Fresh thyme
5 sprigs

Fresh rosemary
5 sprigs

1x Bunch parsley
roughly chopped

Process

1. Preheat the oven to 180C / 350F/ Gas mark 4

2. Place the onions, beetroots, parsnips, carrots and new potatoes in a baking tray.

3. In a bowl, mix the olive oil, balsamic vinegar, honey and garlic.

4. Pour over the vegetables. Using your hands, rub until the vegetables are completely covered with the dressing.

5. Roast the vegetables in the oven for 15 minutes.

6. Tear the thyme and rosemary sprigs over the vegetables. Sprinkle with parsley and roast for a further 15 minutes. Allow to cool.

In your lunchbox arrange a portion of the roasted vegetables.

Bon Appétit !

Gil & Michiko would like to say special thanks to:

black&blum for their support, Yumi Nitta for inspiring visual ideas, Joanna Kamath for the valuable feedback, Spyros Zevelakis for consulting on graphic design, Kfir Malka for helping us with the print work and all our friends who tested our recipes.

Distributed in 2009 by black + blum ltd.
2.07 oxo tower wharf,
bargehouse street, london, se1 9ph, uk
www.black-blum.com

Food styling & recipe consultancy:
Sandra Baddeley